EXMOOR
CENTURY

Hilary Binding • Brian Pearce • Steven Pugsley

EXMOOR BOOKS

First published in 2001 by Exmoor Books
© 2001 Hilary Binding, Brian Pearce, Steven Pugsley

ISBN 0 86183 441 0

British Library Cataloguing-in-Publication-Data
A CIP data record for this book is available from the British Library

EXMOOR BOOKS
Official publisher to Exmoor National Park Authority
Exmoor Books is a partnership between
Exmoor National Park Authority and Halsgrove

Halsgrove House
Lower Moor Way
Tiverton EX16 6SS
T: 01884 243242
F: 01884 243325
www.halsgrove.com

Printed and bound in Great Britain
by Bookcraft (Bath) Ltd, Midsomer Norton

✑ INTRODUCTION ✑

There can be few people who are not fascinated by old photographs. Portraying both people and places, they form a link with the past that offers a sense of identity and continuity that is all too rare in these days of rapid change. They remind us of our roots. These were the men and women and children who lived and worked in this place before we did; these were the sights they saw, the houses they inhabited, the shops they patronised, the buildings in which they worshipped. We have the advantage of them, for few had similar opportunity to know such detail about their forebears as we do.

There is inevitably an element of sentiment in our study of old photographs but they offer the critical viewer so much more. It is no coincidence that every schoolchild now learns to use old photographs as an historical resource. They point up the past at a particular time and invite comparisons with the present day. They highlight change.

In *Exmoor Century* photographs from the past are set beside photographs taken very recently from the same spot. They allow us the opportunity to consider in depth the changes that have taken place on and around Exmoor over the last hundred years.

Many of the photographs have not been used before. Some of the earliest include images of Dunster taken by the pioneer, James Date, who set up business in Watchet in the 1860s as a 'photographic artist' and photographs of Selworthy taken by Robert Gillo of Bridgwater round about 1870.

The bulk of the pictures, however, come from the work of Alfred Vowles, who took photographs all over Exmoor both before and after the First World War. Alfred moved to Exmoor in 1910 and the next year bought a horse-drawn caravan which served as his lodgings and a place to develop his plates. Over the next twenty-five years he travelled to towns and villages all over the moor capturing the sights that he saw. Later he moved into Minehead and took on a host of voluntary activities, most to do with the conservation and care of the moor he knew and loved so well.

Alfred Vowles was interested not only in places but in people at both work and play and many of his photographs, like those of the swimming pool at Minehead, record a way of life that the Second World War brought to an end.

The book also includes photographs from a newly acquired collection, taken in the 1930s and '40s by R.A.J. Bowden (usually known as Jasper). We know little about Jasper; his family may have originated from the Brendon Hills and he seems to have spent part of his life in Sussex. He was a semi-professional, travelling the countryside on his motor bike and taking photographs with the intention of using them either as postcards or magazine illustrations. Even his

Vowles with his caravan at Porlock, 1912

Bowden on his motor bike

snapshots are razor sharp. Jasper Bowden tended to see and record the 'wider' scene – views that many might then have termed ordinary but which today are valuable because they pinpoint places at a particular date. All his photographs are named and dated.

At first glance it could be thought that there has been little change on Exmoor over the last century, apart from the introduction of the internal combustion engine and all that that entails! And there will be people who welcome that idea for there is, of course, a school of thought that considers that conservation means that nothing should be changed and that therefore Exmoor should presumably be set is some kind of time warp. But the foolishness of this idea becomes apparent the moment one tries to work out just when Exmoor reached its zenith – should it be 'preserved' as it was in the Iron Age? Or in the days of the Royal Forest? Or before the internal combustion engine spoiled everything? The truth of the matter is, of course, that Exmoor is changing all the time and the biggest changes are brought about by the activity of human beings.

Certainly there are plenty of places where there has been little change. One reason for this must, of course, be the remoteness of Exmoor, which has helped preserve it from the demands of the outside world. Many villages have been in the care and ownership of landlords like the Aclands of Holnicote, the Fortescues of Filleigh and the Luttrells of Dunster who continued to use local building materials and methods on their estates when all around was changing. In the seaside towns most change took place so long ago that it is now regarded as something worth conserving. Take Minehead, for example, where the town chose to become an Edwardian watering place and its turn-of-the-twentieth-century buildings are now much admired. The occasional eyesore like the building that replaced the old Plume of Feathers can only make us thankful that worse didn't happen.

Today many of the properties that belonged to the Aclands are in the watchful care of the National Trust while National Park planning procedures prevent damaging change in other villages insisting that new houses are built in traditional materials and styles.

Houses and cottages may not have changed much in shape and in the position of windows and doors but most a century ago were plain and foursquare, simply lime-washed with little adornment of any kind and often with a slight air of being uncared for. Today many would not seem out of place in the pages of a glossy magazine for the design and decoration of our homes and gardens is something that we all to some extent or other care about today. There is more money about and more leisure – a century ago hard-working labourers had little time to spend on anything but the essentials.

Even the countryside has altered, albeit subtly. Generally there are more trees about. People no longer cut wood for firing, some marginal agricultural land has been given over to new plantations and ornamental trees have been planted. Dutch elm disease has also taken its toll. In many places field boundaries have been altered to accommodate modern farm machinery and large fields have replaced the traditional small ones. On the high ground areas of moorland were ploughed in the 1950s and in some places conifers planted. Villages have been smartened up, partly to attract visitors, and, in far too many places, 'road furniture' detracts from the rural scene. The motor car has a lot to answer for – thank goodness for the National Park's planning regulations, you might say, or it would be much, much worse. The hazards of taking some of the present day shots were great! It is not a good idea to stand in the middle of the sea front at Minehead in high summer these days even if Alfred Vowles was able to in the 1930s.

This book does not pretend to be a comprehensive survey of Exmoor a hundred years ago. Although there is a spread of photographs from right across the moor some places are not as well represented as others. This will, we hope, be remedied in a second volume. While some pictures are captioned fully, others stand on their own merit for you to enjoy and for you to compare. Part of the fun of looking at old photographs lies in searching out the differences and recalling memories of how things have changed – and if you haven't known Exmoor long there is still plenty here to whet your appetite and help you forge links with the past.

ᔆ ALCOMBE ᔆ

The Britannia Inn, c1920. The Minehead Hobby Horse en route to Dunster. In 1901, the Britannia is said to have been 'a rather dubious public house'. On the day of Dunster Fatstock Show it opened very early and at seven in the morning cattle waited in the street outside while their drivers, from Porlock, Luccombe and Bossington, revived themselves before finishing the trip to Dunster.

The Britannia Inn, c1930. Note the smarter appearance and the remodelled front as the Brit. gears itself to receive holidaymakers.

✀ ALLERFORD ✀

The packhorse bridge and ford at Allerford, c 1870. The photographer was Robert Gillo of Bridgwater. The tree-shaded cottages at Allerford were then owned by the Aclands at Holnicote.

Today trees have been cleared and the whole area opened up. New houses replace the old thatched cottage to the right of the ford in the first picture. In the second picture the rear of Allerford House can be seen clearly. Most of the older properties at Allerford are now owned by the National Trust.

⊱ BRATTON FLEMING ⊰

Post Office c1925 (courtesy Bill Pryor). Before improvements to the A39 the main road from Barnstaple to Challacombe and Lynton ran through Bratton Fleming. Little has changed in this view since the original photograph was taken. The Post Office is still there and next door is the Methodist Church and schoolroom, originally the Bible Christian Chapel, built in 1854. Further down the street towards Barnstaple is the Baptist Chapel, built in 1850. In between is a cottage known as Beara Cross. An old guide book states: 'accommodation is much sought after here on account of the healthy situation of the place, about 900ft above sea level.' Despite its fine views, however, it hardly developed as a tourist resort. The new roads and railways by-passed it and it did not develop further until recently, when new housing estates have turned it into a dormitory village for Barnstaple.

∽ BRENDON ∾

The village in around 1925 by Alfred Vowles. Alfred Vowles lived in Brendon during the early 1920s and, as he took comparatively few photographs of the Devon side of the moor, this was probably taken during that period. The scene has not changed as much as it would appear from these photographs. The East Lyn river still runs as close to the road and houses, except that it is hidden by shrubbery. In *Lorna Doone* the forge at Brendon was so close to the river that the blacksmith cooled his horseshoes in it. The building behind the man who appears to have a pet sheep was the old post office. Across the river can be seen Countisbury Mill but the river is now lined with trees on that side. Brendon is still a straggling one street village. The main settlement was Millslade and it spread along the road to the bridge at Leeford.

Malmsmead Ford c1934. This scene is one of the best known on Exmoor. It shows the ford over Badgworthy Water, which divides Devon from Somerset at this point. The view is looking from the Somerset side to the Devon side, which is in Brendon parish. The house beyond the ford is Lorna Doone Farm, originally Malmsmead Farm. Although it lies in 'Doone Country' the farm appears to have no direct connection with the novel. It was, however, home to the Snow family until they moved to Oare Manor in the eighteenth century and Nicholas Snow was neighbour of Jan Ridd, the hero of the novel. It is undoubtedly old and it is claimed to have Saxon parts. The adjacent Malmsmead Bridge is seventeenth century and a Scheduled Ancient Monument.

It is not clear where the actual Doone Valley of the novel was supposed to be but locals marketed the East Lyn valley between Oare and Brendon as the Doone Valley, as that was accessible to motor coaches. Many visitors came to see the locations in the novel and the farm was leased as a gift shop which, from time to time, has also sold refreshments. Traffic became very congested in the 1960s and '70s and the farm became surrounded by car parks. A survey by Devon County Council suggested contingency plans should congestion become worse. Since then, however, coaches have become too large to negotiate the narrow roads, interest in the story has lessened and visitor numbers in general have dropped.

Rockford Youth Hostel c1925, by Vowles. This is situated across the East Lyn river from the Rockford Inn. Although the building has not substantially altered it is barely recognisable now as large trees hide it completely and there is a high fence around the downstream end. In the old picture it is clearly a Youth Hostel and café. It is accessible via a bridge just upstream and a path runs alongside it between Brendon and Watersmeet. There is no access for cars, although the old ford still crosses the river below. It is currently divided into holiday cottages. It is not clear when it became a Youth Hostel but it still served that function in the 1950s. Apparently the pub across the river was too much of a temptation for some of the young customers and a former warden claimed that it was the girls who were usually the worst for wear afterwards.

Rockford c1890. At the time this picture was taken the settlement and ford were known as Ashford. A guide book of the same date as the photograph describes it as having 'an inn, one or two lodging houses, and a group of cottages on the banks of the East Lyn, which is here crossed by a footbridge.' The inn was Rockford Inn and the settlement subsequently became known as Rockford. The ford crossing the East Lyn originally connected the Brendon road with a steep track winding up through the woods to Wilsham. Below is Ash Pool, one of the deepest pools in the river and formerly well known by salmon fishermen. Upstream was a wooden bridge described as a 'clam' or log bridge when this photograph was taken. The ford is still there and the inn and a more substantial bridge on the site of the old one but the view has changed with the growth of trees on the river banks.

Post Office c1930 (courtesy Bill Pryor). This was taken from near Brendon Mill looking west-wards down the village street. It is in what was once the hamlet of Leeford. The previous Post Office was further down the street nearer the Staghunters Inn. Brendon lost its shop and Post office in the 1990s. The village has become a centre of controversy as 40% of its houses have become second homes whilst locals cannot afford first homes and the community with its facilities is disappearing. Some local traditions remain and a pony fair is still held there on the third Saturday in October. The unsold ponies used to go to Bampton Fair the week afterwards but the market has now gone.

Bridge Ball c1910 (courtesy Bill Pryor). Bridge Ball is a crossing point of Farley Water. Its first mention was in 1685 when Major Wade, one of the leaders of the Monmouth rebellion was captured there. He was sheltered by the wife of a farmer named How and later by a Farmer Birch at nearby Farley Farm, where the capture took place. Until the eighteenth century Brendon church was at Cheriton and most of the parishioners of Brendon would have had to cross the bridge here on the way to church. The church was moved nearer to the main settlements of the parish in 1738 and the hamlet has remained off the beaten track ever since.

❦ BRIDGETOWN ❦

In the parish of Exton, Bridgetown is famous for its cricket ground and its pub. When photographed by Alfred Vowles (probably in the 1930s) it was the Rock Inn, but it was subsequently renamed the Badger's Holt.

☙ BROMPTON REGIS AND BURY ☙

Around 1935, by Alfred Vowles. The inn sign for the George can be seen on the right-hand side.

Bury in the early years of the twentieth century, by Dulverton photographer John German – the ford and packhorse bridge: both should be attempted by modern drivers somewhat gingerly!

⊰ CARHAMPTON ⊱

Looking towards Minehead, c1912. On the left the Butcher's Arms is still thatched while on the right is Roseville, built in c1901 by James Watts, blacksmith and postman. Beyond is Eastern Farm. In the centre background is The Cottage, then a general stores. The modern equivalent, taken early in the morning to avoid the traffic, shows how the paraphernalia of modern living dominates our villages. Several of the farm buildings are now part of the Recreation Centre, while The Cottage, with its façade remodelled, is now a private house.

The Butcher's Arms, c1935, by Alfred Vowles. This inn has been offering refreshment to passers by for nearly 400 years, or more, if the date, 1635 set in sheep's knucklebones in the floor of the bar, is anything to go by. Before the days of village halls it was the meeting place for all village organisations from church vestry meetings to payouts from the friendly society. The unusual inn sign it now displays was made in 1938 by the artist, Rachel Reckitt, who lived at nearby Golsoncott.

The Pound, c1912 (courtesy, Carol Ell). The green under the giant walnut trees was always a popular place to play. The wall surrounded the old village pound where straying stock would be held until claimed. The walnut trees eventually uprooted the wall, which had to be rebuilt. Today street furniture and white lines on the road add an urban note to this village street.

Looking towards Minehead, 1930, by Alfred Vowles. A stone's throw from the station, beach huts offer their delights to the holidaymaker. Cars indicate a wealthier class of visitor but whoever you are you can hire a deck chair and enjoy the sunshine. Now permanent chalets occupy the site, some used for holidays, others providing year-round homes. On the left the signal seems to have shrunk! The Coast Path runs between the chalets and the beach.

The Blue Anchor Inn, c1905. In 1765 this road from Minehead to Watchet through Blue Anchor was designated as one of the turnpike roads of the Minehead Turnpike Trust. It became the usual route to Minehead for travellers from Bridgwater and beyond. On the right, strategically placed with views up and down the roads, is the old tollhouse where tolls were collected from travellers. Behind is the Blue Anchor Inn that may have its origins in medieval times as an inn accommodating the many pilgrims who came to visit the cliff-top chapel of St Mary (now gone). The inn became popular as a venue for political meetings as early as the 1700s and as accommodation for holiday makers soon after. Superficially, the outside appearance of the Blue Anchor Inn is little altered as it continues to provide good accommodation and refreshment. Car parks have replaced stabling and accommodation for private carriages. The former tollhouse has been modernised in popular style with dormer easy-care windows and a garden room with views to the sea

∽ CHALLACOMBE ∽

The village, in 1925, photographed by Alfred Vowles. This picture was taken from near South Lane, which connects the old packhorse bridge at Challacombe with South Regis Common. The view looks north westwards up the Bray valley and over Town Tenement and the Methodist Chapel with its former schoolroom which now doubles as the village hall. Challacombe was known for 'the poorness of its corn harvest and the richness of its turf harvest.' A. G. Bradley recalled the village of slate-roofed whitewashed cottages plumed with peat smoke in the 1860s. In the nineteenth century Devon cattle were used for ploughing and taken along drove roads for sale in London. Each autumn 40 or more Exmoor ponies were led along roads to Bampton Fair. Mixed farming had largely finished by the early twentieth century. Until then oats, plus a little barley and wheat, had been grown as winter feed for the stock. In 1914 sale particulars described Town Tenement as a 'small dairy farm' and Regis Common as 'summering land'. The poor trade for mutton and beef in the years of the agricultural depression led to an increase in dairy farming, which has now disappeared. Now farmers supplement their living from tourism and some of these buildings are holiday accommodation, with a camp site just out of sight to the left.

Challacombe Mill c1910 (courtesy Val Thorne). This view is taken from Mill Bridge over the River Bray looking north towards Challacombe Mill. Richard Huxtable was once the miller at Challacombe, where he died in 1855. He was principal millwright for the area and his diary from 1824-5 survives. His son, Richard, later ran the village pub and his other son, William, took over the mill. An account suggests that the mill and pub were close to one another, so perhaps there was another mill which has now completely disappeared, as the pub is a mile away.

The known mill was shown as a corn mill on the 1905 OS Map. It stood closer to the river than the present house and hardly a stone remains. The wheel had a tree trunk for an axle, timber spokes and all the machinery had timber cogs. Traces of a small mill building used for livestock and a leat were recorded in the 1980s. The leat still runs over the top of a grass field, drops over a shoot and flows past a row of former cottages now used as farm buildings before running into the Bray. There was a sizeable hamlet around the mill.

The Black Venus c1935. Formed by joining two seventeenth century cottages, the Black Venus was mentioned as early as 1812 but the name may have referred to a nearby cottage and meadow. A little later it was known as the New Inn and, when the church bells were rehung in 1845, it was renamed the Ring of Bells to celebrate the event. It was part of the Fortescue's Challacombe Estate and doubled as a small farm. Field Marshal Montgomery and Harold Macmillan stopped there for cream teas. Ring of Bells was the commonest pub name in Devon and in 1967 the landlord changed it to reduce confusion with other pubs. He wanted a unique name and chose one with a local connection. There is a story that it was named after a sheep that nobody could shear, and another that it was named after a carving in dark local stone.

∞ COMBE MARTIN ∞

The Beach, c1920. The harbour at Combe Martin is hardly used now but old pictures show how it was frequented by quite large sailing vessels running across the Bristol Channel. This picture is entitled 'coal boats' but the same boats were used for a variety of cargoes. Both domestic coal and 'culm' for burning limestone were brought from South Wales. Although Combe Martin had its own limestone quarries for producing agricultural lime, a purer form of limestone was brought from South Wales for burning in harbour limekilns to produce lime for mortar, plaster and limewash. This was just dumped overboard and picked up from the beach by horse and cart. The boats had keel boards to stabilise them at low tide, when other cargoes were taken off rather precariously by wheelbarrows on gang planks. In June and July the same boats would take local strawberries back to South Wales.

Seaside, c1910. This picture is probably older than it has been dated. Some postcards were used for many years with the same pictures. About the time this card was dated the harbour lime kiln, which had been the subject of a famous picture by Turner, was demolished and replaced by a coastguard station, now a café. The River Umber runs under the main street and issues under the bridge above the horse and carriage. It ran a mill in the group of buildings above it. The building with the ornate gable was Sea Croft Boarding House apartments.

Victoria Street, c1910. This picture is also probably older than it has been dated. It shows part of Combe Martin's main street, which runs for about a mile and a half and is reputed to be the longest village street in the country. The street changes name seven times, showing its gradual development as it linked the two settlements of Head Town and Seaside. Head Town, where this picture was taken, running between the church and manor of Buzzacott, seems to have developed first and Victoria Street was continuously built up by the seventeenth century.

By the mid nineteenth century many of the old cottages had become slums and Charles Kingsley described Combe Martin as the 'mile long man sty'. Both agriculture and mining were in recession and there are many such accounts. A suggestion was that one of the main land-lords deliberately put rents up and allowed cottages to fall into disrepair so that he could force tenants out and redevelop. Hence the demolition of some of the older properties in this picture as the village developed with tourism and market gardening. Beside the inn, Pig's Lane ran down to cross the Umber and serve large limestone quarries and kilns on the far side of the valley. The George and Dragon Inn has now moved down the road nearer to the church and a newer building three doors down has become the Lion Hotel.

∽ COUNTISBURY ∾

The Blue Ball, c1910 (courtesy Bill Pryor). The Blue Ball has been an inn since the sixteenth century and was well known in coaching days, when the coaches would stop for a change of horses after the pull up Countisbury Hill. The coaches continued running up the hill until 1921. The inn sign of a blue metal ball can be seen hanging from the left hand corner of the building. In the 1990s it briefly became the Blue Boar after a change of ownership and extension of the building. The post box remained where it was but incorporated into the new wing. It is now known as the Exmoor Sandpiper, but locals still refer to it as the Blue Ball.

Watersmeet c1900. Watersmeet is the confluence of the East Lyn and Hoaroak Water (sometimes known as the Combe Park Water at this point). It lies in a gorge nearly a thousand feet deep, surrounded by ancient oak woodland which is now a Site of Special Scientific Interest. Watersmeet House was built as a fishing lodge by the Rev. W. S. Halliday in 1832. The area is still popular for fishing, now controlled by the Environment Agency, but the salmon, trout and sea trout are by no means as numerous as they were. Halliday was inspired by the Romantic Movement in the arts both in the design and setting of the lodge and by a poem by Wordsworth, written for his sister Mary, which is inscribed above the doorway. The materials for the house were mostly quarried or cut from the woods nearby. The lodge formed part of the large Countisbury estate which has remained in the same family since but much diminished in size.

The National Trust now owns Watersmeet and has been gradually acquiring land in the area since 1934. The house is now an information centre and café and is a tourist 'honeypot'. It was very popular when the earlier picture was taken and subject of many postcards. The main difference is in the bridges. The earlier bridges were 'clammers' or log bridges, piled sometimes on supports of loose stones. Presumably, they were replaced each time the river flooded, as there seem to have been many versions. They gradually became more substantial but, since all were washed away in the flood of 1952, the bridges have now been constructed higher above the water and in a manner so that they break away instead of damming the river in a flood.

Brendon Post c1925. The photograph by Alfred Vowles shows the A39 looking westwards from its junction with a minor road from Brendon. To the right of the road is Wellfield House, now hidden behind a high beech hedge. The house has recently changed ownership for the first time in many years and until then it had changed little from the Vowles picture. In the distance is Kipscombe Hill. As part of Countisbury Common, the heathland here was mostly reclaimed in the early 1960s, when reclamation was generally running at a fast pace on Exmoor. The heathland in the foreground was reclaimed earlier. The coastal heath is naturally well drained and is relatively easy to reclaim, so areas like this were particularly vulnerable. This type of heath is now rare and the National Trust has plans to restore it on parts of Kipscombe Hill which were reclaimed as recently as the early 1980s.

The Village c1910 (courtesy Bill Pryor). Countisbury today is just a few cottages a church and an inn. There was little development in the parish in the twentieth century except perhaps for the widening and improvement of the A39, the traffic and the car parks. Large parts of the parish now belong to the National Trust. The church, which changed much with the growth of the community in the eighteenth and nineteenth centuries, has changed little since. From 1854-56 its curate was the Rev. W.H. Thornton, who described the parish in his book *Reminiscences and Reflections of an Old West Country Clergyman.* He spent much of his time improving the school and teaching. The little schoolroom has survived intact as it was when it was eventually closed in the middle of the twentieth century.

∽ CUTCOMBE ∾

The Wheddon Cross part of the parish around 1912 by Vowles. The Rest and Be Thankful Inn boasts a pillared portico, the roadway is unmetalled and a tailor's shop occupies the bay-windowed building on the right (now a private house).

Again, pre-First World War, by Alfred Vowles. The view from the school looking towards the inn. One wonders if the bicycle on the right was what carried the photographer to the village.

❧ DULVERTON ❧

The Ancient Order of Foresters gather outside the Union Workhouse in Dulverton, c1907. The Workhouse, established in 1855 (and costing £2811 to build plus £675 for the site) was closed in the early 1930s. The building became the headquarters of the Dulverton Rural District Council in 1960. But upon that body's demise in 1974 (when West Somerset District Council took over its responsibilities) the new Exmoor National Park department began its occupation and the building was re-christened Exmoor House.

Bridge Street, the first photograph dated to before 1900. On the right is the Boot Inn. The second photograph is dated 1904 and everything looks more pristine and prosperous. The cottage on the centre-left was destroyed by fire in 1918. The site was eventually occupied by a garage as can be seen in the photograph from the 1950s – a tribute to the ever-growing importance and presence of the motor car.

High Street, around 1900. The Ellerton's Stores building replaced a single-storey police station. After the Stores moved to Fore Street, it became a cycle shop, bank and finally a chemist's.

High Street, looking towards Bridge Street, around 1900. The Lamb Hotel, on the left hand side, was converted to flats in the 1980s.

Looking up Fore Street, around 1900. On the left are Bayley the grocer and draper, and Follett the saddler (in the present Post Office building). On the right hand side is the Market House, which was reconstructed in 1927 as the Town Hall by Professor (later Sir) Albert Richardson, who gave it its trademark double flight of steps.

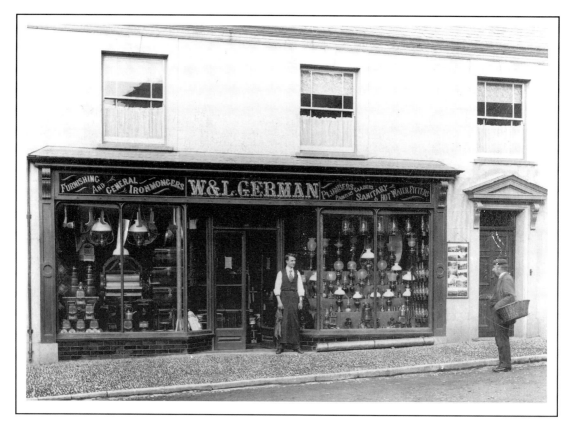

German Brothers, ironmongers, pre-1914. Founded in 1847, the business continued until 1991, when the premises were acquired for use as a library and information centre on the Fore Street side. The Dulverton Heritage Centre at the rear occupies the former storage rooms. At the time of the Germans' departure the stock still included coffin plates for the paupers at the Workhouse.

Fore Street from Bank Square, around 1890, before the Lion Hotel gained its portico and gable.
When its then proprietor, William King, sold up in 1888, the property had '16 bedrooms, coach
houses, lofts, granary and stabling for 35 horses'.

Northmoor Road, looking towards Lady Street, around 1900, showing one of several bridges over the leat.

Battleton, the genteel suburb of Dulverton, prior to 1914.

⊷ DUNSTER ⊷

The High Street, c1868. A quiet morning in Dunster. On the left the Luttrell Arms, once the guest house for the Abbot of Cleeve Abbey and later cottages, is the venue for local meetings and the best inn providing for visitors in the area; the Yarn Market has long outlived its function as a focus for the woollen industry. We can date this photograph almost exactly because in the background scaffolding surrounds the towers of the castle. In 1867 when George Luttrell inherited he employed the distinguished architect, Anthony Salvin, to remodel the castle as can be seen in the modern photograph, with the new towers and service wing on the left. The open street, once the venue for weekly markets, now parking lots. A garden now occupies the former space in the foreground of the old picture, hence the new photograph being taken a few feet in front of it to avoid obscuring bushes!

Dunster Castle, c1868. Demolishing the old east wing prior to building Salvin's new service wing. In 1976 Colonel (now Sir) Walter Luttrell gave the castle and gardens to the National Trust who look after it today.

The West Somerset Foxhounds arriving in Dunster, c1935, by Alfred Vowles.

Dunster Water Mill, c1930. Seen from the castle grounds, by Vowles, this unusual Domesday twin-wheeled mill was little used in the early twentieth century and was a favourite haunt of artists and photographers. Leased by Laura and Arthur Capps in 1979, the mill was restored to working order and is now open to the public. Trees now shade the wheels from the path through the gardens.

Rose Cottage, c1920. This picturesque corner of Dunster is always popular with visitors. The road leading to the ford and packhorse bridge was once the main route to Carhampton. Careful ownership over centuries by the Luttrell family followed by direction from the National Park Authority mean that this corner of Dunster is little changed. Dutch elm disease has claimed trees but flower gardens are equally well tended.

This photograph by James Date was taken about 1865. It shows St George's church and, on the left, a drapers that later became Dunster Supply Stores. The Amor family ran the shop at the end of the nineteenth century and in 1901 it was taken over by Mr J. Parham and sold almost everything under the sun! For the next eighty years and more it was known as Parhams. Today it sells antique linens, a link with its origins.

Alfred Vowles photographed Locks Tea Garden in its heyday in the 1930s. Then the shop at the front sold sweets and chocolate and tickets for visiting Dunster castle garden. Situated behind a house that was once used as the village school, both shop and Tea Garden have seen a variety of uses. Today it is once again a place of pleasant refreshment.

❧ EXBRIDGE ❧

The settlement of Exbridge has the distinction of straddling two counties, the bridge marking the boundary between Devon and Somerset. This picture was taken on the Devon side before 1914.

⊙ EXFORD ⊙

The White Horse Inn, beside the bridge, c1895. Immediately to its right, across the Green, can be glimpsed the village's other inn, both run by the Tarr family. A very elegant street lamp stands on the left of the bridge.

Tarrs' Family Commercial Inn and Posting House, c1895. It is now the Crown Hotel. The building to the left still houses the village stores. It is noteworthy that the Village Green was walled at this date.

The Village Green, probably in the late 1940s, by R.A.J. Bowden.

Another view by R.A.J. Bowden from the late 1940s, showing the Blacksmith's Cottage, centre right, which was so badly damaged in the 1952 Lynmouth Flood that it had to be demolished. It is said that the flood waters carried the saddles from the White Horse Yard into the house.

Stable Corner, by R.A.J. Bowden in the late 1930s. The absence of tree cover and of development on Church Hill in the far distance, are striking.

Stockleigh Lodge, photographed by Vowles probably before the First World War. The building was subsequently extended, from 1919 onwards, the work occupying almost the entire inter-War period.

Higher Thorne Farm, captured by Vowles around he late 1920s, or early '30s. The farm, at one time a property of Neath Abbey in South Wales, was purchased by Matthew Waley-Cohen (a well known Exmoor figure, County Councillor and High Sheriff of Somerset) in 1951 and he extended the house to the south with a substantial new wing.

⤳ HAWKRIDGE ⤝

Hawkridge is one of those typical Exmoor communities where at first sight little seems to have happened over the last century, but where there has, in fact, been a number of subtle changes. In the first view from the church tower of around the 1920s there is no Village Hall and the cottages at the top of the picture stand in an intact row. By the early 1950s, the two cottages nearest the road have all but fallen down and the Hall (built 1937/8) has appeared.

The pictures on the right are details of the 1950s photograph on the previous page. Today, the Old Post Office in the foreground has been extended, the Old School has gained dormers, the Old School House has an extra storey and to its left are the two Whiterocks Cottages built in the mid 1950s.

Rowe Farm, probably in the 1930s. Standing to the east of the church, Rowe had become so dilapidated and unstable by the 1940s (hence the buttresses) that it was reduced by a storey and the front wall completely reconstructed.

Hawkridge School (right) and School House around 1900. In the middle stands William Lock, who carried on the family trade of carpenter here, begun in the 1840s; in his turn he was succeeded by his son and grandsons who still operate the same business from the same premises – possibly a unique survival. Certainly the Lock family (by whom the photographs in this Hawkridge section were loaned) are a superb source of local historical knowledge. The school closed in 1955 and was subsequently converted into a house.

The Blacksmith's Shop, circa 1900.

The row of five cottages known as 1-5 High Street. Now just one house, used as the village Post Office, the remnants of the two left hand cottages are now garages.

The Village Hall under construction in 1937/8. The Hall was the gift of Colonel Eustace Harrison who had bought virtually the whole of the parish from the Herbert Pixton estate.

East Hollowcombe Farm, by Vowles around the 1930s. Whiterocks Cottages now stand before the Old School House on the left of the picture.

The Devon and Cornwall Brigade Camp on Anstey Common in 1908. In many respects the picture is more interesting for the buildings of West Hollowcombe Farm in the right foreground : the thatched farmhouse was demolished and replaced by a new house (somewhat to its right), built at the same time and in the same style as the Village Hall in the late 1930s. Col Harrison who instigated both, had the roofs red-tiled rather than slated because he believed that this looked more akin to thatch.

Lower Willingford Bridge by Alfred Vowles, probably in the 1930s. The road surface is rough, and the carriageway gated – as motor vehicles increased and stocking rates rose after the Second World War, cattle grids became a more convenient alternative on roads from moorland to cultivated ground.

∽ LEIGHLAND ∾

Leighland Chapel, c1859 (courtesy Glyn Court). This chapel at Leighland, part of Old Cleeve parish, may have been Saxon in origin. During the medieval period it was served for a while by the monks at Cleeve Abbey. It survived the Reformation and in 1611 Robert Poyntz left money for its maintenance while in 1685, Prudence Poyntz arranged for it to be served by a Benedictine chaplain with a stipend of £7 a year together with food and lodging and a horse. In 1791 we learn from Collinson that it was '46 feet long and 19 wide with a small turret and one bell' and it also had a singing loft. During the mid-nineteenth century, iron mining on the Brendon Hills attracted many people to the area. In 1865 the chapel at Leighland was completely rebuilt at a cost of £1200 to cater for the growing population. It had seating for 220! The yew tree looks as if it pre-dated the new church by centuries.

⌐ LUCCOMBE ⌐

The Square, c1900. This is the hub of the village; on the right the path through the lychgate leads to the churchyard and the medieval church of St Mary the Virgin. Disastrously altered in 1840, a more sensitive restoration in 1895 repaired some of the worst excesses. In the centre of the picture at the foot of Stoney Street is Church Gate Cottage with, at the far end, a long room with a large leaded window. This room was the village school before 1881. The schoolteacher lived in the cottage. Note the window guards designed to prevent the casement windows being opened so wide that they were in danger of being knocked off by passing carts. On the left is Ketnor, the village post office and stores. The schoolroom is now used as a parish store. The post office is no more. The window guards remain.

Looking north from the Wootton Courtenay road, c1910. On the left is Ketnor. The houses on the right were built in about 1905 to replace a row of thatched cottages. Beyond Church View with its thatched roof, semi-circular bread oven and date over the door, 1680, is the only survivor. In the distance the trees shade the village school, opened initially in 1881 with the support of the Acland family at Holnicote; it re-opened in 1892 following the provision of free elementary education. The modern view is a good example of how much things have been 'tidied up' in our villages over the last century. The village school was closed in 1946 and became first a men's club and then the village hall.

⊷ LUXBOROUGH ⊷

The Methodist Chapel, Kingsbridge, c1935 by Vowles. Access to the Methodist chapel, opened by the Bible Christians in 1858, was by way of a bridge over the stream. Above the entrance a tablet read 'Preach the Gospel to every creature.' The building was almost square with the usual preaching desk facing six or seven rows of benches and a gallery with three long forms. There were six separate sets of hatpegs and a brass memorial to Sammy Coles, indefatigable lay preacher, 'the Billy Bray of the Brendon Hills.' In 1981 church membership was down to seven and a few years later the chapel was closed. The bridge remains in place but gloomy evergreens now mask the spot where the air once rang to Charles Wesley's hymns.

Kingsbridge, c1930. This was a busy crossroads, again photographed by Alfred Vowles, with inn (the Royal Oak on the left), post office nearby and general stores which in 1935 was kept by Annie and Rosa Scott. A large blue enamel sign, recently discovered on a building plot opposite the shop, may date from before the First World War. It reads:

VICKERY
GROCER DRAPER HATTER
TAILOR & BREECHES MAKER
SPORTING AMMUNITION ETC

The inn remains but shops and post office are gone. The lime-washed plaster has been stripped from the houses leaving the soft sandstone open to the elements. Across the road open land is now crammed with new houses.

☞ LYNMOUTH ☜

East Lyn Valley c1930, from the Vowles collection. These photographs are taken from the East Cleave above the East Lyn gorge. Lynmouth, down in the valley, appears to have shrunk but this is only because trees now hide many of the buildings. The scar of the A39 at Watersmeet Road, constructed in 1837 is now, at last, hidden. The gardens at Middleham at the bottom of the picture are now also hidden. Prior to the 1952 flood disaster there were ten cottages along the path here, with their backs overhanging the river. All were washed away and several lives lost. The gardens have since been kept up as a flood memorial.

The side of Hollerday Hill above Lynton also looks more bare in the old photograph. In the wooded part can be seen the ruins of Hollerday House. The house was built for publisher Sir George Newnes in 1893. He died there in 1910 and three years later the house burned down, supposedly as a result of arson. In 1933 the hill and ruins were purchased by John Holman and given to the town as a pleasure ground. The ruins became a play area for children and after the Second World War they were blown up to make them safe. Prominent also in the old picture is the large block of the Royal Castle Hotel to the front of Lynton above the West Lyn gorge, which descends from the left of the picture. This was also burned down under mysterious circumstances in the 1980s and there are proposals to rebuild it as a block of flats. In the new picture can be seen the development along Grattons Drive above and to the left of Lynton.

Lynmouth from the Tors 1896. The old photograph was taken from the Tors on the ridge between Countisbury Hill and the East Lyn gorge. The exact viewpoint has scrubbed over and is no longer accessible as well as being private. In 1885 William Bevan leased the Tors estate from the lady of the manor. By the next year he had built the Tors Hotel in a prominent position and was advertising fifty building sites on what he called Tors Park under the 99-year lease. This sparked a heated debate between some visitors who thought the landscape was being desecrated and some locals who thought of the developments as improvements. The *Lynton and Lynmouth Recorder* of 1888 congratulated Mr Bevan in 'sparing no pains in making the Tors Park, which was formerly a barren waste, into what might be described as a paradise of loveliness...' At the same time a travel writer wrote: 'A long and grievous gash has been torn in the side of the beautiful hill opposite Lynmouth – a gash which must leave behind it a broad deep scar never to be healed.' One can see from the pictures, however, that the scar of the newly cut cliff railway in the old picture has been disguised by the growth of trees which has spread over the surrounding allotments and up over Hollerday Hill above.

River Lyn, c1930. This pair of photographs shows not so much the effects of the 1952 flood but the flood protection measures taken after it. The old Drill Hall to the left of the river was not destroyed by the flood but demolished to re-route the river. Remaining on that bank is Rock House, just out of the picture to the left. Lynmouth Street runs just out of the picture to the right. Prior to the flood it was the only street on that side of the river. The new Riverside Road was constructed where the course of the river had been to help protect the main part of the village from the river and to relieve traffic congestion. The river bed was widened and a wide bank added to accommodate any future flood of similar proportions. The old Lyndale bridge was hidden by the trees in the old picture. It had a span of five metres, inadequate for the flood waters. The new one was made with a span of 24 metres and is more prominent. Restoration works took many years and the new bridge was finished in 1957. The roof of the lifeboat house can be seen at the bottom of the old photograph. This was destroyed by the flood and replaced by the Flood Memorial Hall. Currently it contains a model of the village as it was before the disaster.

Lynmouth from Summerhouse Hill c1950. This picture, taken shortly before the flood disaster, appears to be taken from the air but was taken with a telephoto lens from Summerhouse Hill above the junction between the East and West Lyn gorges. It shows the mouth of the River Lyn and its delta. The main changes between the two photographs were brought about by the flood prevention measures following the disaster of 1952. It is also noticeable how much more traffic there is and how the number of pleasure craft in the harbour have increased. The harbour itself is now protected by a much more substantial wall to deflect the river water. On the far side the old pier and the Rhenish Tower on it were demolished by the flood and a more substantial pier was built with a replica of the tower. The tower was originally built to hold a tank which supplied running sea water to baths in the Bath Hotel, the substantial building to the left of each photograph. It was probably built around 1830 but later embellished to make it look more attractive. Some said this made it look like a tower on the Rhine and the name stuck, although its constructor, General Rawdon, is supposed to have imitated a picture of a tower on the coast of what is now Lebanon. In the old picture one can clearly see the remains of old causeways and breakwaters on the delta. The main one on the left bank of the river has now been consolidated and extended to allow passengers access to pleasure boats at low water.

Mars Hill c1890, (courtesy Ilfracombe Museum). Mars Hill was once the only way up to Lynton from Lynmouth harbour. Until the early nineteenth century there were no roads as such to Lynmouth, just tracks. The road up Lynmouth Hill was made in 1813. The Esplanade had not been constructed and the harbour was only accessible via Mars Hill. The white building on the left is Manor Cottage, which was a tea room in the earlier picture, now a shop. A rock projected from under the cottage into the harbour and the Esplanade later had to be constructed around the rock, pushing the course of the river further to the east. Some of the rock still projected into the river mouth in 1952 and this helped deflect the waters in the flood disaster, so that Mars Hill remained unscathed. Hence there is little difference in over a hundred years between the photographs. The cottages were originally fishermen's cottages and cellars for smoking herrings. The cottage of which the roof appears above the tall house at the top of the hill is Shelley's Cottage. Early in the nineteenth century this cottage belonged to a Mrs Hooper. The poet Shelley and his teenage wife Harriet stayed with Mrs Hooper in 1812 but it is not clear whether she owned this cottage during that time. The whole block of cottages is now in the same ownership and the cottage is part of the accommodation offered by the Rising Sun Inn.

∽ LYNTON ∽

Barbrook c1920, (courtesy Bill Pryor). The first account of a bridge here was in 1678 when 1s 4d was paid for the repair of 'Barbereck mill bridge'. The hamlet appears to have been quite industrial at the time with tucking and fulling mills for the woollen industry, which faded in the late eighteenth century, leaving Barbrook an agricultural hamlet. A guide book of the 1850s describes the journey from Parracombe to Lynton: 'The wild and open district, through which the road generally passes, is relieved by wood, rivulet and fertile meadow; a scene much heightened on reaching Barbrook mills, where nature and art are so pleasingly united as to produce a picture of more than ordinary beauty.' Here the three main tributaries of the West Lyn meet. Following the 1952 flood disaster the river now runs in a 25ft wide channel between banks twice as wide to accommodate any future floods.

Barbrook c1930, from the Vowles collection. This scene was taken from an old track which ran up from Kibsworthy Farm at Barbrook. The Post Office is there now and the track has been blocked by the building of a new house. The scene is still recognisable but Barbrook was changed greatly by the 1952 flood disaster. Twelve people lost their lives and great damage was done there. The main road ran past the Methodist hall and schoolroom in the top left of the picture and turned down through a narrow gap between the cottages and over the arched bridge. On one side was an old forge and on the other side a shop. The bridge was washed away by the flood. It was temporarily replaced by a Bailey bridge and now a footbridge. In 1956 the main road was re-routed to cross the river on a wide concrete bridge upstream at Barbrook Mill. The hall, forge and shop are now private houses.

Cherrybridge, Barbrook, 1904. This was a very popular scene in its day and was reproduced in various forms by several publishers. It was used as a general rural scene as well as an Exmoor souvenir but the Exmoor horn sheep firmly locate the picture. The bridge crosses the Barbrook at its confluence with the West Lyn, which runs to the left of the picture. The road running up Ilkerton Hill was the old road from Lynton to South Molton, running over the Chains and now becoming a dirt track beyond Shallowford. The scene is still recognisable today but the setting has changed with the busy A39 running by and a petrol station on the other bank of the West Lyn, where a weir used to divert water to Barbrook Mill.

Town Centre c1930, from the Vowles collection. Lynton grew rapidly with the tourist industry throughout the nineteenth century. The main boom came towards the end of the century. By the 1880s the regular visitors were complaining that the new building was spoiling the scenery. With the construction of the cliff railway in 1890 Lynton expanded rapidly from its original centre around and below the church westwards towards the Valley of Rocks. Building filled in the former meadows between Lee Lane and Lydiate Lane, with several new parallel roads running between. However, the steam had begun to run out before construction of the Lynton and Barnstaple Railway in 1898. Sir George Newnes, financier of the railway, had decided against building a pier in 1892, causing a drop in property prices and a collapse of the building industry. He continued financing local projects, including the Town Hall in 1900. This can be seen to the right of the picture. The Methodist Church to its left was built in 1910 and is now a cinema. The resort had been a genteel one until the 1890s when the influx of trippers did not suit the wealthier visitors. After the First World War the resort became more 'downmarket' and there was little more change to the centre of the town. The 1980s brought a considerable depression to the town and attempts are still being made at a revival.

Lynbridge c1910 (courtesy Bill Pryor). The view looks up the West Lyn valley from a track through Lyn Wood which runs from the Lyn bridge to Summerhouse Hill. Alongside the river is the row of cottages ending in Lynton Mill, then described as a corn mill. It was, however, built in the eighteenth century by and for a builder who used it as a sawmill. Some of the timbers used in Lynton Town Hall were cut there and it continued in use until the Second World War. It became unworkable following the 1952 flood. At the other end of the row is the old smithy and blacksmith's cottage, alongside which was a weir across the river to divert water for the mill. Beyond the row is the Cottage Inn, now Ye Olde Cottage Inne. Above this is the footbridge built to replace the old packhorse bridge destroyed in the flood. The main block of cottages to the right of the picture is alongside Lynbridge Road, running down towards Lynmouth Hill. Above is Lynway and near the top of the hill is Station Hill, running up to Lynton Station. The view cannot be repeated today because of the growth of trees in Lyn Wood. However, the cottages are still recognisable, although the mill is now Mill Cottage, a private house, as is the smithy, now Forge Cottage.

Railway Station c1930, (courtesy Bill Pryor). The station is situated well above Lynton town and, despite many proposals to extend the railway to the town, there were coach services linking it with Lynton and its hotels. It was the terminus of the narrow gauge railway from Barnstaple opened in 1898. The railway was financed by publisher Sir George Newnes, whose wife cut the tape at the station at the opening ceremony. The line was taken over by Southern Railways in 1923 and the station extended. The station master's accommodation, which included first floor bedrooms, was converted into offices and he was built a new bungalow on the bank opposite. Behind the photographer's viewpoint was a goods yard with engine shed and coal and water stores. Staff consisted of a station master, warehouseman and porter (two in summer). When the line was closed in 1935 the station building fetched £475 as a private house. It now belongs to a railway enthusiast who has a large collection of memorabilia.

The Valley of the Rocks from Hollerday Hill c1910. These pictures illustrate how the nineteenth century desecration of the Valley of Rocks continued into the twentieth century with the further improvement of the road and the addition of the roundabout and the car park. Since the 1970s there have been many suggestions for the reduction of through traffic and removal of the roundabout, car park and picnic site. The latter was constructed with the toilet block by the National Park Authority to replace an even more unsightly static caravan park. Many trees were planted to hide the cars in the picnic area but most did not survive in the exposed conditions. Trees have, however, survived and grown behind the cricket pavilion and bracken now swathes the once bare screes. The cricket ground was levelled in the 1890s and the pavilion, thatched until it was burned by arsonists in the 1990s, is now a Listed Building.

The Valley of the Rocks c1910, (courtesy Bill Pryor). The wall in these pictures encloses what is now the tea gardens. The present café is reputed to be an eighteenth-century hunting lodge of the de Wichehalse family of Lee Abbey, former Lords of the Manor and owners of the Valley of Rocks. In 1799 the poet Robert Southey said the Valley of Rocks was: 'a spot which, as one of the greatest wonders of the West of England, would attract many visitors if the roads were passable by carriages.' A year later the then Lord of the Manor set about the enclosure of the valley in speculation for the impending boom in tourism. The wall around what is now the cricket pitch enclosed the rabbit warren and it is likely that the café was then the warrener's cottage. A magnificent Bronze Age stone circle and Iron Age settlement near where the round-about is now were robbed of stones for walls and gateposts. The track which meandered through the valley was made into one broad curve.

Hoaroak Farm 1896, from the Oldham collection. It is not clear when Hoar Oak Cottage was built. The first accounts of it are from 1839, when it was owned and farmed by John Vellacott, who also owned North Furzehill and Ratsbury. With Hoar Oak he owned two blocks of rough grazing of 140 and 146 acres. Frederic Knight probably took a lease on the land in 1861 and on the cottage six years later, putting in a shepherd for Hoaroak and Chains herding. After Frederic's death, Viscount Ebrington bought the cottage and 60 acres from a Mr Jeune for £1150 in 1898. The cottage has clearly been extended lengthwise and this was probably undertaken at this time, when the range in the cottage, marked 'Castle Hill' (Viscount Ebrington's estate) was probably installed. A Scottish shepherd, James Johnstone, was put in the cottage in 1886 and died there in 1904. It is probably him in the photograph.

The last of the Fortescues' shepherds was Abe Antell, who was moved to Blackpits in the early 1950s. The 5th Earl Fortescue and his wife died in 1958, leaving no direct male heir. Parts of the estate were broken up and sold off. Hoaroak and Chains herding passed through two owners before being sold to Somerset County Council in 1969. Hoaroak was then let on an agricultural tenancy. The National Park Authority gutted the cottage some time in the late 1970s. Army helicopters were used to carry roofing materials out to the site. At the time the cottage was largely intact but now the flooring was taken out, the windows blocked up and the natural slate roof replaced by a corrugated one. The intention was to make it safe to convert into a bothy-type walkers' shelter and still is if funding becomes available.

Lyncombe Farm lay partly in Lynton parish and partly in Brendon but the farmhouse and buildings were firmly in the former. The farmhouse pictured in 1927 was virtually destroyed in the 1952 Lynmouth Flood and the steading was never re-occupied. Now only a few stones and some occasional walling mark its site.

❧ MARTINHOE ❧

The Church, 1899 from the Oldham collection. The church at Martinhoe is dedicated to St Martin, although the name of the village seems to pre-date the church. The oldest parts of the present church are the chancel, dating from the late thirteenth or early fourteenth century, along with some of the fabric of the nave and tower and a piscina. In the early nineteenth century the congregation outgrew the church, which was enlarged and heavily restored between 1866 and 1867. The children in the picture are in the yard of the National School, which was opened in 1873 at the instigation of the Throckmorton family, for a long time Lords of the Manor and owners of most of the parish. Previously the church vestry, built in 1851, was used as the schoolroom. The parish population in the late nineteenth century was much higher than it is now and the school has long since closed.

Beyond the churchyard is the church house. Such buildings were particularly suited to large rural parishes where parishioners could rest and take refreshment after their long walk to church. They became meeting places and often doubled as the parish hall and village pub. This one backs onto the churchyard. It became Hollowbrook Cottage and has been converted for accommodation for the Rectory, which is now a guest house. The Rectory was built in 1800 and when it served the Rector the cottage was used for stables and accommodation for the groom. It is mostly modernised, but retains an old chimney stack and eleven pigeonholes. It could date from medieval times.

Hunter's Inn c1870, (courtesy, Ilfracombe Museum). This scene was taken from Churchway Path and cannot be reproduced today because trees have grown around the track. The whole scene has grown leafier. One can see through old photographs how the hillside behind the inn gradually changed from furze to bracken to scrub and woodland.

The inn was a simple thatched cottage until the 1860s. At the time it was customary for fox shooting parties to walk over the cliffs from Combe Martin, it being impossible to hunt the cliffs with horses and hounds. The owner was in the habit of keeping a barrel of ale to refresh them before their long walk back. The cottage was then enlarged sideways, called an inn and began to rent rooms. As tourists came to the area the inn was considerably enlarged with a two storey extension to the rear. In 1895 the whole was burned to the ground. A story goes that all that was saved was a barrel of beer that was brought out in flames but intact. The inn was rebuilt two years later in the Swiss style fashionable locally at the time. It became popular with parties of students from Oxford as a place to read and write during their holidays, but after the First World War the wealthier visitors did not return and the place was more frequented by trippers. The writer J.H.B. Peel lived and wrote in the former staff annex in the woods adjoining the inn during the 1960s.

Woody Bay Station c1910, (courtesy Bill Pryor). The station is adjacent to Martinhoe Cross, on the A39. At just below a thousand feet above sea level, it was at the summit of the narrow gauge Lynton and Barnstaple Railway. It was built to serve the proposed resort at 'Wooda Bay', three miles away. Land for the station was donated to the development company and it was intended eventually to build a branch line to the resort. The venture failed and the station was never very busy. The line was opened in 1898 and the name changed to Woody Bay in 1901. At its height the narrow gauge, single track railway carried 100,000 passengers and 8000 tons of freight per year. A porter was laid on in summer for the visitors. The station house was a simple chalet design with a booking office, office and ladies waiting room. Gents, presumably, had to wait outside.

The line beyond the station ran through a cutting bridged by the A39 and the road to Woolhanger. The cutting has now been filled in and the A39 bridge removed. When the picture was taken there was a woodland to the left, between the station and Station Hotel, which is now Moorlands holiday flats. Under the Act of Parliament which enabled the railway the company were obliged to construct Woody Bay station and 'forever efficiently maintain' it. The line was closed in 1935 and the station sold a couple of years later for £425. It became a private house but was used only occasionally as a holiday home and was little altered. The railway preservation society has now bought it and has started work on putting in modern facilities so that part of the line can be re-opened from there towards Parracombe.

∾ MINEHEAD ∾

North Hill, c1880. This view of North Hill reflects the days when agriculture and sea faring were at the heart of the town's economy. A shingle ridge separated sea and land. On the lower part of the hill the North Field, in medieval times an open field, slopes to the sea. The ancient strips of land can still be identified. At the foot of the hill lies Quay Town, home to sea captains and fishermen. To the left of the flagpole are the coastguard cottages built in 1877. In 1887 Elgintower was the first house to be built on the open slopes of North Hill with many others following during the first decade of the twentieth century. In the early twenty-first century trees crown the hill, some planted and others allowed to grow, no longer needed for fencing and firewood. In the foreground on the left is the Metropole Hotel, first built as the Esplanade Family Hotel in 1893. A sea wall protects the land from flood.

Minehead Harbour c1900. The harbour is busy with ketches and fishing boats. The steam crane used for unloading coal and other goods can be seen in the centre of the picture. A short railway allowed it to move along the quay. The thatched building in the centre is the customs house and on the right and left are cellars and warehouses.

In Quay Street, before 1910. The Red Lion was rebuilt in 1902. Note the houses on the right

In Quay Street, soon after 1910. The houses on the right were badly damaged by the 1910 storms and were eventually pulled down as part of a road-widening scheme.

Beach Hotel, c 1905. The Beach Hotel was built in 1875 after the coming of the railway. It was a popular hotel for families and for sporting visitors, some of whom brought their horses by train in order to hack and hunt. Hackney and other carriages waited for incoming trains and were available for hire for short journeys and by the day.

The Promenade c1905.

On the Beach, c1950, by R.A.J. Bowden.

Again, around 1950. In the background of the modern photograph is Butlins and the 'Dome'.

The Swimming Pool, 1930s. The swimming pool, one of Mr Geoffrey Luttrell's enterprises, was made to Olympic specifications and opened in 1936. National Championships were held on occasion. After the war the pool was bought and managed by a consortium before being sold to Butlins. It was demolished in the 1970s. Flats are now being built on the site.

The Wellington Hotel, before 1873. The Duke of Wellington Inn was built in 1820 and pulled down in 1893 to make room for a new temperance hotel. It was a posting house, and during the nineteenth century posed a real threat to the Plume of Feathers on the opposite side of the Square. This photograph was taken before St Andrew's Church was built in 1880. Note the crowd of people watching in Bampton Street where there was a bakery.

Kinnersley's, c1885. Built as accommodation over the shop sometime after 1873, this building was at different times a music shop, a general stores and, for some years until 1913, the Post Office. On the right are the first houses on the right hand side in Park Street. Note that they just stop! On the left is the Wellington Inn.

The Plume of Feathers, Wellington Square, c1912. Once Minehead's most prestigious hotel, it accommodated political meetings, hunting parties and holidaymakers until its demise in c1965. In this picture onlookers and riders wait for the arrival of the hounds.

Looking up the Parade to the Plume of Feathers, pre-1870. On the right is the old Fish Market with myrtle-clad houses built after 1791 to replace the houses that were burnt during the fire of that year.

Looking up the Parade, c1885. On the left is Stuckey's Bank built before 1869. The trees indicate a new civic pride.

Looking up the Parade, c1930. From 1869 until 1903, new buildings replaced old. On the right the new market house was completed in 1903 – it retained its clock turret – and together with the new Stuckey's Bank, now NatWest, were the last buildings to arrive. The wide street was, before the 1791 fire, crowded with old houses.

Looking down the Parade, c1925. On the right is Floyds, established as a drapers at the foot of Friday Street in 1877.

Looking down the Parade, c1950.

Looking down the Parade, c1960.

2 Park Street, c1930. The Minehead premises of the *West Somerset Free Press* under renovation. The newsagent and booksellers was usually known as Cox's and accommodated a circulating library.

Friday Street, 1926. With the coming of the motor car, garages sprang up quickly, Capron and Sons in the Parade being the pioneers. Bradbeer Bros. were trading in Friday Street before 1928. In the early 1930s they advertised as district agents for Austin cars, sold motor-cycles and were wireless experts. They had garaging for 70 cars. The premises is now a furniture shop, a branch of Hatchers in Taunton.

Quirke's Almshouses, c1900. Robert Quirke, merchant and churchwarden, gave these almshouses to the town in 1630. The income for their upkeep came by leasing two cellars on the quay which in 1910 became St Peter's Chapel. The houses are built on the site of the old market place and the stump of the market cross can be seen beside the gas lamp in the centre left. They have been brought up to modern standards and so have lost their Listed Building status.

Blenheim Terrace, c1880. Designed by Piers St Aubyn, 1871-1873, these were some of the earliest houses in Minehead built to accommodate visitors. The Terrace was extended by local watchmaker turned builder, John Brown Marley, between 1896 and 1901.

Looking down the Avenue, c1900. Behind the trees on the right is the Minehead Tannery.   The Methodist Church seen on the left was built in 1871 and extended in 1886.   On the left is Seaview House.

Looking down the Avenue, c1930. Taken from a slightly different angle, this photograph shows Minehead Hospital, opened in 1920 in the building put up in 1889 as the Town Hall.

❧ NORTH MOLTON ☙

East Street, c1890. East Street is the main street of North Molton, running down from the Square to the bridge over the River Mole. The street no doubt extended down the hill as the population rose with the booms in the mining industry in the early eighteenth and mid-nineteenth centuries. During the latter period the population rose from 1500 to 2000. The village became a town and borough. People came and went with the fluctuations in the mining and woollen industries. At times accommodation was cramped, conditions were insanitary and outbreaks of disease were common. When the industries were depressed and the harvest bad many died and the parish did what it could to look after its poor. It had its own workhouse and charities provided poor relief for people in their homes and almshouses, some of which can be seen on the right of the picture. Nearby was a chapel. Both miners and farm workers were strong non-conformists and John and Charles Wesley preached in North Molton, John at least three times. Today the village is largely a dormitory of South Molton and Barnstaple. Sheep farming has been the dominant industry for the last hundred years and the parish boasts one of the highest densities of sheep in the country, sheep outnumbering people by at least 50:1.

Hunt Meet, the Square c1890. The view is taken looking westwards across the Square, which is still very recognisable. In the far corner is the vicarage, behind which, out of view, is the church. Running to the east of the church was The Lawn, where Lord Poltimore had his kennels. The Lords Poltimore, the title of the Bampfylde family, owned two mansions by the church: Court House and Court Hall. At this time at the lower end of the Square was a smithy which was reputed to have been the workshop of the legendary Tom Faggus before he became a highwayman in the style of Robin Hood. He turned to crime after a failed lawsuit with one of the Bampfyldes.

Heasley Mill c1890. The view looks northwards from the road down from North Molton. To the right is the wooded Mole valley where many old copper mines were situated. These kept working until the late nineteenth century and sent ore down the Mole valley to South Molton and thence to Barnstaple. When the Bampfylde mine closed some thirty to forty cottages in the hamlet were left empty and pulled down. Until then the hamlet had housed 200 people. Lord Poltimore gave every encouragement to his tenants to keep the remaining cottages in good repair.

  Running alongside the Mole from a weir near the Bampfylde mine was a leat which ran the large mill in the picture. This was shown on maps of the time as a corn mill. It was recorded in the seventeenth century as a grist mill but was adapted and enlarged in the late eighteenth century for weaving woollen cloth by adding on a huge four-storey workshop. This came at a time when the local woollen industry was declining. Water-powered mills could not compete with the steam driven machinery of the north and this one survived until the 1850s. For a time the workshop was used to accommodate miners and a miners' chapel was constructed a little up the road but the workshop was demolished soon after the mines closed and the original mill returned to grinding corn. It is now a dwelling. Right under the hill was the smithy and a little up the valley to the left was the school where there is now a public car park and toilets. Behind the row of cottages were the parish allotments.

∽ OARE ∽

As photographed by Vowles, probably around the time of the First World War, this most romantic of churches has an almost blasted appearance, with the trees severely trimmed.

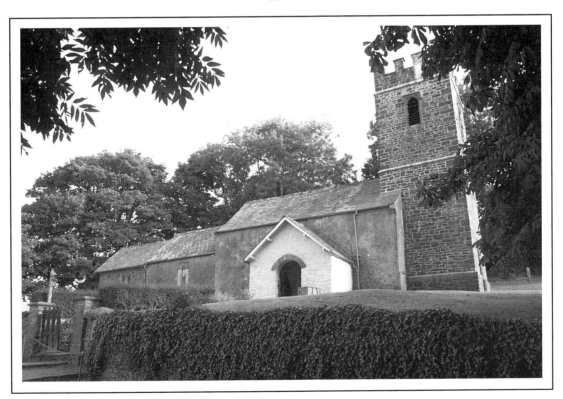

∽ PARRACOMBE ∾

The Fox and Goose, 1892, (courtesy Sally Dallyn). There has been an inn on this site since the sixteenth century. The photograph shows the inn in the year it was burned down. At the time it belonged to Henry Robert Blackmore, second cousin of novelist R.D. Blackmore, and formed part of the Blackmore Estate, which included Blackmore Gate.

The inn was served by stage coaches which ran between the railway at Barnstaple and Lynton from 1860, linking with a service between Lynmouth and Minehead which started in the 1850s and ran until 1920. Henry Blackmore resisted the building of the Lynton and Barnstaple Railway through his estate, petitioning against the act of parliament which gave approval to the route in 1895. As a result the spelling of Blackmoor Gate was changed when the railway station was eventually built there. The present inn was built in 1894. Parracombe was by-passed by the A39 in the early 1930s and the railway closed in 1935, losing even more trade for the inn. It survived the 1952 flood disaster when the bridge over the Heddon, which runs alongside the inn, was washed away.

∽ PORLOCK ∽

Doverhay Manor Museum, Porlock

J. Ridler & Son, Boot and Shoe Makers, c1900. The Ship Inn is on the left with Ship Cottages in the background. Direction signs on the house point to Lynmouth and Porlock Weir. The large sign advertises Exmoor Pharmacy of Minehead where Mr Culverwell A.P.S., chemist, also made artificial teeth. There was no chemist in Porlock at that time so Mrs Ridler kept a cupboard with various items normally stocked by chemists. Ridlers later opened a shop in Park Street, Minehead that still bears their name.

Doverhay Manor Museum, Porlock

The arrival of the stagecoach from Minehead at the Ship Inn, c1900. Two extra horses were added here for the steep journey up Porlock Hill. A complete change of horses was made at Culbone Stables for the rest of the journey to Lynton. Red Rose Cottage in the background was the home of George Hawkins, shoemaker. In the modern view, new houses in the background are part of Pollard's Court.

Doverhay Manor Museum, Porlock

The heavily laden stagecoach just above the second bend on Porlock Hill, 1898.

Doverhay Manor Museum, Porlock

The old Post Office and shop, c1900-1910. Behind the wall on the left was an orchard where the present Methodist Church was built in 1927. The thatched building beyond was a farm, which was sold in 1910, and a row of shops built in its place. The Post Office now occupies the building on the right.

Doverhay Manor Museum, Porlock

The Castle Hotel, c1900-1910.

Doverhay Manor Museum, Porlock

Parson Street, c1880, looking down. The houses were demolished soon afterwards in order to widen the road, and to open up the view of the church. The only building recognisable today is the old Rose and Crown, centre. Overstream Hotel is on the left and the churchyard on the right.

Doverhay Manor Museum, Porlock

The High Street c1900 showing the Wesleyan Chapel built in 1837 and the Lorna Doone Hotel built in the latter part of the nineteenth century. The Countryman Restaurant now occupies the old Wesleyan Chapel.

Doverhay Manor Museum, Porlock

View of the east end of the High Street, c1880. The large porch and window on the left is where the chemist's shop is today. The thatched building, centre, was the Three Horse Shoes Inn, replaced by the Lorna Doone Hotel. The only recognisable building is the Royal Oak.

Doverhay Manor Museum, Porlock

Dover Court, c1880. The railings are still in place. The cottage on the left was demolished in c1950 to become part of the car park. The only other feature unchanged is the Royal Oak Inn. Dover Court is on the right, part of Doverhay car park on the left. The houses on the left were built in 1897.

Doverhay Manor Museum, Porlock

View of the village, c1900. Notice the many elm trees around the hedgerows. The church steeple can be seen on the right, the tannery building on the left. The large double barn with an iron roof was the bark shed of the Tannery.

(vertical text along right edge) Doverhay Manor Museum, Porlock

High Street looking towards Doverhay Corner c1900. The sign on the left advertises a Horse Omnibus service. The house on the left with a large window was burnt in 1928. It stood at what is now the entrance to England's Road. Part of what is now the museum, Doverhay Manor House, can be seen in the centre distance.

The centre of Porlock, c1905. This photograph was taken from the window of the house that is now the Overstream Hotel. Opposite is the thatched Rose and Crown with Cape's grocery shop on the corner. To the left is Fox Fowler's bank. On the right the row of shops includes Stenners and Burgesses, both bakers and S.S. Stenner, greengrocers. Hedges surround the churchyard and a solitary gaslight lights the corner. The Rose and Crown is now a private house and Cape's has gone. A row of shops still serves the village though some are now catering specifically for visitors.

St Dubricius, Porlock, 1890. The shingle spire of Porlock church under repair during the restoration of 1890. The nave roof was renewed at the same time. The house in the foreground which is being demolished was once a bakery. Note the bread oven on the right.

❧ RALEIGH'S CROSS ❧

The inn (inscribed Hotel over the doorway) about 1935. The inn stands on one of the main routes into Exmoor and is of long standing. It throve particularly during the era of Brendon Hills mining in the mid-nineteenth century when it and the inn at Heathpoult Cross were the nearest licensed establishments to the miners' colony.

❧ SELWORTHY ❧

The lane to the church, c1912, by Alfred Vowles. On the left is Selworthy Cottage, built in 1825. Note the view of All Saints' Church, and the cottage garden in the foreground. The plantations on the hills behind were made by Sir Thomas Dyke Acland in the nineteenth century to mark the births of his children. Trees and hedges now obscure much of this view.

Holnicote House, east front, 1785-1851. The Acland family of Killerton in Devon and Petherton Park near Bridgwater acquired the Holnicote estates at Selworthy when Thomas Acland married Elizabeth Dyke of Tetton near Taunton in 1745. In 1779 the house at Holnicote was burnt to the ground and a few years later a new house was built on a slightly different site.

Holnicote House, west front, 1785-1851. This charming house was also burnt to the ground in August 1851.

Holnicote House was rebuilt in 1861. This photograph taken in the late nineteenth century shows the south front and west end before the games room/ballroom was added.

Holnicote House, early twentieth century, showing the south and west elevations. In 1941 yet another fire destroyed the thatched roof at Holnicote. The Holnicote Estate was given to the National Trust by Sir Richard Acland in 1944. Today the house is occupied by the Holiday Fellowship.

Periwinkle Cottage, Selworthy Green, c1920s. Selworthy Green was remodelled by Sir Thomas Dyke Acland in the late 1820s. Former farmhouses were adapted to provide accommodation for long-serving retired servants. Thatching on the left is Arthur Kingdom who started work as a thatcher for the Holnicote estate in 1919. Standing is, almost certainly, Jimmy Groves who was a general handyman on Selworthy Green and who was not averse to being photographed if his hand had been 'crossed with silver!'

Now in the care and ownership of the National Trust, Periwinkle Cottage is best known today for its cream teas.

Ivy's Cottage on Selworthy Green, c1875. This picture was taken by Robert Gillo who worked as a photographer in Bridgwater. It is possible that the picture shows Nanny Downs, who lived there until she was ninety. The Cottage was named after Ivy Cann who lived there until recently and who devoted herself to looking after the parish church and greeting its many visitors. The house is now in the care of the National Trust.

Dunkery from Selworthy c1930, again by Vowles. In the middle distance lies the village of Luccombe. Porlock Vale is a patchwork of small, hedged fields with elms prominent in the hedgerows. In the 1970s and '80s hedges were torn out and fields put together to accommodate modern machinery. Although the policy has now been reversed this landscape demonstrates what has been lost – in many cases large fields have replaced the traditional small ones. Dutch elm disease has also taken its toll.

☙ SIMONSBATH ❧

Hoaroak Sheepfold 1896, from the Oldham collection. The sheepfold in Long Chains Combe appears to date from the days of the Royal Forest, when shepherds from surrounding areas stayed there most of the summer with their flocks, renting the grazing. It may date from the eighteenth century, when the Acland family leased the Forest from the Crown. It was purchased from the Crown by John Knight in 1818. In the 1841 census we hear of four of John Knight's Irish labourers being housed at Hoar Oak in Exmoor parish. This cottage was probably built in the 1830s and was derelict by the 1851 census. In the Knight accounts there is a mention of it being thatched in 1835. One suggestion is that it was in Long Chains Combe but another places it on Hoar Tor. The sheepfold, however, clearly had living accommodation with it, the remains of which can be seen in the old photograph. The Chains herding, originally based on the sheepfold, was probably run from there until Frederic Knight, John's son, took the rent of Hoaroak Cottage in Lynton parish in the 1860s to house the shepherd for the herding. Presumably the sheepfold became derelict at that time.

South Molton Road c1910. The view looks north eastwards down the Barle valley from an old quarry in the Deer Park across the valley from Cornham Brake. In the distance can be seen the edge of Simonsbath with West Cottages on the Challacombe Road and Simonsbath Barton above them. It can be seen clearly how the Barton has grown as the home farm for what is now the Astrop Farms estate, which was part of the Fortescue Estate in the earlier picture. At the time the photograph was taken the whole area was part of the Fortescue estate and parts of the Barle valley were being developed for forestry, which never dominated the landscape. It is the hedgerows which have now grown up to make the scene leafier and the sides of distant Lime Combe have scrubbed up.

Simonsbath Village c1890. This is one of a series of pictures from the same viewpoint. It clearly shows the mansion behind Simonsbath House which John Knight started building in the 1830s and never finished. He had planned to demolish parts of his house in the Midlands and incorporate them into his new house. He gave up when his anticipated inheritance of a Midlands estate failed to materialise. He retired to Rome in 1842 and the shell of the house was eventually demolished in 1899.

Also to be seen in the picture is the old Forest pound under Birch Cleave wood. This long pre-dates the Knight era and was used for impounding farm animals which remained on the former Royal Forest outside the times permitted for pasture. It fell into disuse when John Knight purchased the Forest in 1818 and at the time of the photograph it was being used as a smallholding by the owner of the post office. There are now proposals to restore it through bids for European funding.

Brendon Two Gates c1925. This is a well known Vowles picture showing the county boundary wall at Brendon Two Gates. The wall was built in the 1820s for John Knight. He had just bought the Crown's allotment of the Royal Forest of Exmoor following an Act of Parliament for its enclosure and physical enclosure with this wall was part of the agreement. Here it divided the Knight estate from Brendon Common. There was a local practice at boundaries of open land to keep the stock from straying by a double gate system. Two gates would be hinged on one post with a knocking post between them at the other end. That way, whichever way the wind blew one gate would remain closed yet both gates could easily be opened without dismounting from a horse. Hence the origin of the name. Until the First World War gypsies would often camp here. The road was widened and metalled in the 1930s as part of an employment scheme during the Depression.

Pound Cottages, around 1900; they were among the very earliest houses in the village, as listed in the 1841 census. Behind the wall on the left is a turf rick – turf being an important fuel – whilst the man in front is posing with a barrow used for moving the turves.

Simonsbath Post Office by Vowles, c1910. The Post Office and stores remained here at Jubilee Villas until the late 1960s.

The Exmoor Forest Hotel, by Vowles c1910. Originally known as the Refreshment House, and then in 1887 as the William Rufus, it became the Exmoor Forest Hotel in 1901. For a time it was split into two, with the part nearest the road being the Temperance Hotel, until re-united in 1909.

⚬ TIMBERSCOMBE ⚬

View over the village, 1935, by R.A.J. Bowden

☙ TRENTISHOE ❧

Cottages, Trentishoe Combe 1904. When A. G. Bradley stayed at Trentishoe in the late nineteenth century he found his accommodation very cold and bare, with the plainest of furniture. The house had a wooden barricade around it which was filled with gorse in winter to protect it from the snow. There is little snow here nowadays and the Heddon Valley is very sheltered and warm. At first sight the cottages in the pictures appear to be much the same but a close look shows them to have been substantially altered. They are now desirable residences and their current value is inflated by their location.

To the left a signpost points up Trentishoe Hill to the church and the road to the right leads to Hunter's Inn. Behind runs Heddon's Mouth Wood. The surrounding land now belongs to the National Trust. In the left hand cottage lived Harry Westacott, a National Trust employee and regular at the Hunter's Inn who died there in the 1980s. The area once had many orchards and in Harry's memory the Trust planted Harry's Orchard, just below the cottages, with local varieties of fruit trees.

❧ WINSFORD ❧

The Royal Oak Inn, around 1910, with an impressive collection of motor cars. In *Exmoor the Riding Playground of England* Cecil Aldin wrote : 'Originally the Oak was just a small village public house and only since the stag-hunting revival has it catered for holiday visitors.'

The Royal Oak by Vowles probably mid-1930s. The inn looks somewhat less prosperous at the tail end of the Depression years.

The Garage around 1935 by Alfred Vowles. Now Thorn Cottage.

A panorama of the village in the late 1930s by R.A.J. Bowden.

⥤ WITHYPOOL ⥢

The Royal Oak Inn by Alfred Vowles, probably about 1920. The photograph was taken, as the caption says, for the sake of the magnificent flock of Exmoor sheep being driven through the village by farmers on horseback observable in the middle distance.

A photograph by R.A.J. Bowden, probably of the mid-to-late 1930s. A horse appears, but the growing importance of the motor car is underlined by the presence of A.A. and R.A.C. signs fixed to the inn's walls.

Raymond's Cottage, as seen by Vowles between the First and Second World Wars. The cottage was rented by the author Walter Raymond for about ten years from 1905, for a shilling a week. Raymond immortalized the village in his *The Book of Simple Delights*.

The village pictured by Vowles probably in the 1930s. Certainly the spot from which he observed this typical Exmoor community was taken over by the Dulverton Rural District Council for council houses constructed about 1950.

As viewed from the site of the Village Hall by Bowden, perhaps on the eve of the Second World War, Withypool still had a working school (left), shop, Methodist chapel (centre left), church and inn. Although the appearance of the village is much the same today the school has closed and the chapel has been converted to a private house. Whereas before 1945 'you had to be paid to live in Withypool' (as one local once put it) by 1990 only 58 per cent of the population were economically active whilst 42 per cent were retired.

From the east, around 1920, photographed by Vowles. There are few buildings to the left of the river, where now former council houses, housing association houses and the village hall snake their way up the hill towards Hawkridge.

Post Second World War, photographed by R.A.J. Bowden. The increase in tree cover is striking. The hedge in the foreground field is in the process of disintegration.

Ferny Ball, above Landacre Bridge, by Vowles, prior to the Second World War. After the War the house was burned out, but the farmstead became the location of the caravan home of Hope Bourne, the Exmoor author and commentator. Although the pattern of the landscape is much the same, it is noticeable that significant parts of it have been 'improved'.

⸂ WOOTTON COURTENAY ⸃

The centre of the village, before 1910.

ACKNOWLEDGEMENTS

The authors gratefully acknowledge the help and assistance given by: Heather Burnett-Wells; Dennis Corner; Glyn Court; Stan Curtis; Sally Dallyn; Doverhay Manor Museum, Porlock; Carol Ell; Ifracombe Museum; Tom and Michael Lock; Mrs Lyddon, Brenda Massie and the Dulverton Heritage Centre; Roderick Milward; Isabel Richardson; Val Thorne and Bill Pryor.